BLOOMING IN WINTER

Jennifer O'Neill Pickering

Poetry Selections
1978–2014

I Street Press

Blooming in Winter © 2014 by Jennifer O'Neill Pickering

Cover art: Jennifer O'Neill Pickering
"Amaryllis," watercolor, "8.5 x 18"
"Woman with Sunflowers," digital collage, "8 x 11"

Interior art by Jennifer O'Neill Pickering in order of
appearance: "Amaryllis," watercolor, "8.5 x 18"
"Three Faces," watercolor, 6"x 18"
"Blue Nude," water color digital enhancement, "12 x 14"
"Young Woman with a Red Bird," watercolor, "11 x 14"
"Summer Garden Spirit (or Goddess)," water color, d. "18 x 18"
"Vase with Sunflowers," detail, watercolor, original,"12 x 18"
"Woman with a Green Thumb," chalk pastel on paper, "26 x 30"
"Women with Sunflowers", water color digital collage, "8.5 x 11"
"Bearded Iris," detail, water color, original, "4 x 10"

Author's photograph by Stephanie Keale Mackey

Book design by Marrowstone Design

ISBN: 978-1-941125-51-9

Library of Congress Control Number: 2015952913

This collection of poems spans several decades. Though writing is a solitary effort, participation in the following writing groups and organizations have supported and strengthened my work: The Sacramento Feminist Writers Guild, The Writers' Circle, Thursday Writing Group, Third Sunday Writers Group, Cache Creek Writers' Workshop, the Sacramento Poetry Center, and Sacramento Metropolitan Arts Commission. Finally, thanks to publishers who provide a home for my writing and to friends, and family for their support.

Acknowledgements

Grateful acknowledgment is made to the following publication in which these poems previously appeared.

Heresies vol. 6 Coming of Age, "Sock Relations"
Poetry Now Online, "First Husbands," "Dawn in Senlis."
The Sacramento Anthology: 100 Poems, "Paper Prisoner"
Suttertown News, "Paper Prisoner " (First prize)
News and Review, "Children Are Like Rivers," "Impromtu Prophet,"
    "Adaptation," formerly published as "Change"
Open Circle, "I Am The Creek"(site-specific sculpture by artist
    Les Birleson)
Tiger's Eye: A Journal of Poetry, "Cadenas d' Amour," (Love Padlocks)
Restore/Restory, "Conversations"
Cosumnes River Journal, "Lucky Girl," "First Harvest"
Sable and Quill, "First Harvest"
Yoga Stanza, "Blessing" appeared as "Blessed"
Earth's Daughters, "Middle Age Lament"
Countylines, "Two Dawns and One Afternoon in Tierra Buena"
Moon Mist Valley, "Two Dawns and One Afternoon in Tierra Buena,"
    "The Tree"
Occupy Wall Street Anthology, "Spring Proverb"
In Retrospect, "Crann," "The Apron," "Blessed or Blessing"
Yellow Silk, "Goosefleshed Spring," "Track Talk"
WTF, "Three Buddhists"
Sacramento Voices, "Three Buddhists," "I Am the Creek"
Medusa's Kitchen, "Fly Fishing," "Trio," "Dream Memory"
"Under Her Marble Gown"(poem play), "Sock Relations,"
    "Gooseflesh Spring"
Room of Our Own, "Gooseflesh Spring"
The Voices Project, "Grandma Bessie,"Three Questions to a Daughter"

Table of Contents

Chapter 1 **Crann**

Aliso

What is called Aliso
California sycamore
Platanus racemosa
is a mother who cradles shade
a tailor of golden mantles
fathering immense stillness
moved by the strings of wind
neighbor reaching across the road
infuctescence of spherical fruit
autumns of selfless giving
in transition smoothing rough layers
shares the same roots with a twin
befriends rivers and land that's low
seeks wells of truth
explores darkness
to great depths.

Crann

More trees than Paris
shade of infinite joy
marriage of earth and sky
rungs to paradise

The house was chosen for
the old sycamore the city gave away
branches grown yard to yard
touching tentatively as new lovers.
The house is simple in design
made of bones of trees--a sacred place.

Her ancestors cradled apple saplings coming west
purchased at nurseries in Missouri and Ohio
precious as the heirlooms left behind.
These they'd plant with raised barns
for pressed cider potent as whiskey.

As a girl she lived on an island of yard
surrounded by oceans of trees whose
April blossoms spun dreams.
The apricot, a favorite to climb
flatten limb to limb
match its shape.

When the developer uprooted
the almond orchard across the road
one linked with a swing,
she wept for hideouts dug
in leafy shade roofs of scrap wood
wattle of mud and Johnson grass

refuge gone in a day.

It is Never Too Late to Climb Trees

sit cross-legged in the air
rooted to earth
anchored to the sky
to trust in another
to break your fall
take another's shape
older than first memory
cause friction
climb to disks of sun
trust in your own strength
balance
on the avenues of squirrel
embark on junkets of clouds
dream
with creatures of song
add to their choir
await the rain
receive gifts of flowers
bows of leaves
tied with fruit
crowned by moons
wrapped in the eiderdown of stars.

Drought

Mary has cut down all her trees
complains to me of my
Crepe Myrtle's messy purple petals
the walnut's errant nuts
sycamore's leaves the size of hands or "stars," I offer.

An unexpected cold
rouges my cheeks
north wind musses my hair
deposits tree's gold
in vaults over my neighbor's fence.

Irreverent, scatters across crushed volcanic rock
mulches the Muhly Grass
green waste overruns the drought tolerant garden.

She shoulders her leaf blower
sends copper and gold packing across the border.
But on August days that fry an egg on pavement
she parks her minivan under their shade.

When Trees Write

They use alphabets of
verdigris, copper, and lime

burrow below the surface
make good use of tables,

fill ringed notebooks
with dissertations on climate change,

never have writer's block,
are breaths of fresh air,

listen to the turtle
dove's coo, persevere,

pause each winter,
resist mildew and worm,

dot their eyes on scrolls of bark,
are lovers' valentines,

dip in inkwells of sky,
outline the rain viridian,

burn leafed folios in fall,
rewrite them each spring,

consult the moon,
edit under lanterns of stars.

Snow of Seeds

With the spring Equinox
arrives the snow of seeds
delivered in four directions
on labor of winds
midwives of coyotes
bobcats rhyme of creek.

Ascend banks of sedge
wade in wild oats
cresting over alder bones
the dreams of sleeping snakes
find the deer's trail
repeated etch of *Vs*
take no comfort
in the blackberry's barbed embrace
difficult and sweet

Climb to higher ground
stand with Cottonwoods
soft wood, unsuitable for lumber
food for the hungry
when granaries went empty.

In shadowed lace
revisit curiosity
curl leaves into Teepees
dance with Kachina dolls
carved from sacred roots
gather bark for bitter teas,
cool fevers
weave saplings into baskets

carry blessings to the trees.

The Oak Tree

opens envelopes of leaves
to be read by the sun and moon.
Leans on air and into wind.
Conserves, but is plentiful in fall.
Thrives even with a heart of wood.
Is uncomplaining without a limb.
Gives birth to another with no regret
and life to those not of its kind.
Holds its ground.
Keeps ordered records
without computer, numeral, or alphabet.
Names the yoga pose.
Lives in both earth and sky.

The Twins at Grist Mill

They are chopping down
the twin oaks at Grist Mill,
seedlings when the track homes were farms
where jays' blue siren of song
echo the drum
of the beaver,
twitch of coyotes' ears
herding pups to sanctuary
in stands of elderberry
Long Horn Beetles
cocooned sleep.

Spring mists disperse
reveal a formable adversary:
Army Corps of Engineers
tromp of steel tipped boots
imprints that aren't forgiving
armed with structural plans
for river channelization
Katrina sloshing dangerously beneath
brims of their hard hats.

Distant rumble of bulldozers
lift the mallards into uncertain flight.
The buzz of chain saws polished teeth
bite weathered flesh.
The final solution
delivered in caravans
of dump trucks,
levees raised
blacktopped
paradise lost.

Bones buried without ceremony
in cemeteries of aggregate.

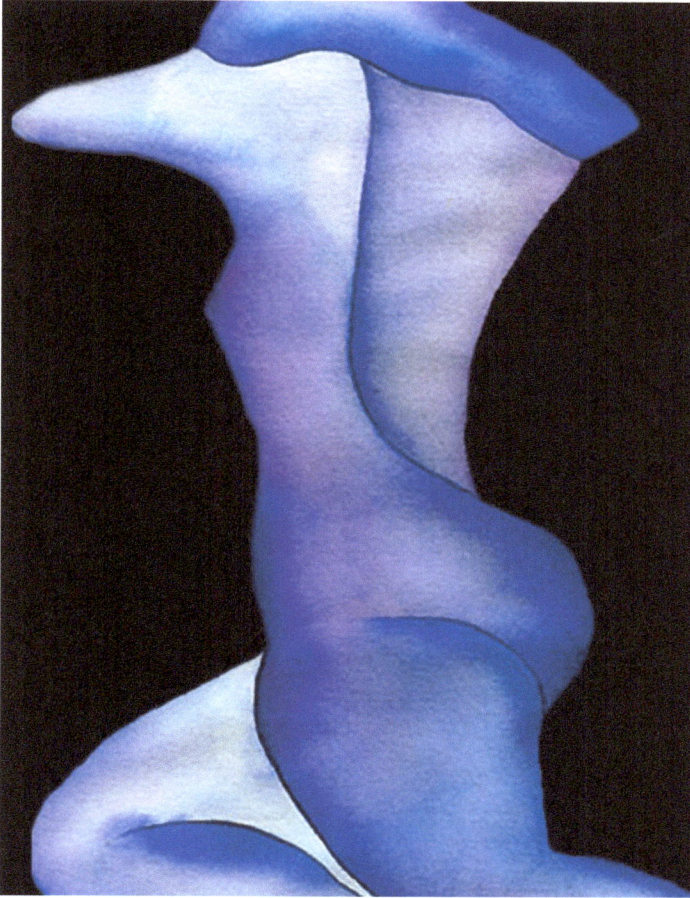

Chapter 2   **Cadenas d'Amour**

Cadenas d'Amour (Love Padlocks)

She hasn't had her heart broken
moped around with blood-shot raccoon eyes,
slammed doors, pounded pillows,
sponged the stream of tears.
She doesn't think she's going to die or wish them dead,
is not on the rebound, had a one night stand,
doesn't ignore the text message,
isn't taking a Facebook break,
still thinks the music on her iPod eases heartache,
has good appetite: isn't bingeing on junk food,
demolishing cartons of cookie dough ice cream,
watching tear jerkers,
stuffing, starving, sublimating pain.
She's in Paris, purchases a love padlock
from a vendor on the Pont des Arts,
makes a wish for good fortune in love
attaches the lock to the bridge's railing,
tucks the key in a safe place.

Anger Chant

You will not furrow my garden again.
The pansies petal carnivorous teeth,
roses wait, fists of barbed wire.
Honeysuckle you loved to drink
grows a noose that fits your neck.
You rot the fruit, spray pesticides,
poison my roots.
Keep Out!
The gate is locked.

Pas de Deux

Linked hands they climb the ridge
above quilted fields farmers sow
mesas flat as table tops
to Cottonwoods marooned in shadow
a place the locals call "Lover's Leap"
and mothers warn daughters never go
improvise ballet
sous sous, pirouettes, adagios, tombes
lift pas de deux toward pastel sky
stretch on white bars of clouds.

Redlands

A Santa Ana has blown away the gray
Birds of Paradise wing air
sweet with orange blossom.

It is an afternoon for
peeling clothes
You turn to me
I let down me hair.

Waves of freeway surf
spill through open windows.
We swim
toward each other's arms.

First Husbands

Like you, Mother, I
elope with a soldier
to Reno, though mine wasn't a good dancer
like my father, who made you dizzy
on West Coast swing.

Good talkers, each could sell a used car without brakes,
Each one, Irish, German, ill tempered, prone to drink.
Yours grew sick of farming, of overalls,
tractor dust in his face,
children sewn in the hem of your skirt.

You thought of leaving.
He's the one who did—to Mexico with the waitress.
Did what you'd imagined but could never do.
In this I'm unlike you, Mother.

Left him the protesting vet with the G. I. Bill,
flashbacks from an undeclared war
the engineer suspicious of change
a penchant for punching walls—me around.

Despite woman's consciousness, the therapy,
I stayed too long.

Reason to Smile

If I could trade the alarm clock
for the cock's throaty cock-a-doodle-doo
gather lupine whose bonnets swell in April wind
by brooks that sing in alto
leave this steady stream of traffic spewing foul perfume
barefoot walk on blades that cause no wound
crowd days with fat cows' moos
paint iris eyes slumbering in beds you tend
slip on floors waxed by moon
toward the warmth you kindle
I would have reason to smile.

She Loves Her Husband's Face

for his beard;
the color of weathered wood,
of earth after rain,
because a smile lives beneath.

In summer the husband tames the bear
with scissors, comb, and care.
For winter grows it long and wild
to keep him warm.

His nose she's drawn a hundred times
and gotten the curve just right.
It bobs above currents of mustache
from which lips find hers.

His eyes are like a walk on the river's trail
linked with sycamores and oak
resplendent with copper leaves unspent
and Sierra streams with stones flecked with gold.
Drop one into a well and you might know their depth.

Off Tahoe Trail

fallen pine lightning struck
rests on fans of tendril fern.
Moss grows a slow green rug
we kneel upon as if to pray.
Folded clothes form pillows
our heads sink into like sun to clouds.
I mount the saddle of your palms,
hold your heart between my arms.
We find our pace this afternoon—and stride.

Gooseflesh Spring

In the mornin' she slipped into white underwear
declarin' the day in rose embroidery Day a' Rest.
Mama tried to tell her ripened thighs freed fail to
fill any desire larger than pursuit a' bad skinned boy
man talkin' Okie, bulgin' neath peg-legged jeans,
kickin' gold dust at a matador. Spring found her
body played with musical fingers strumming the girl
sounding the cord of the woman whose rhythm and
blues steamed windows in a van painted neon. Love
was sweet blend of cigarette breaths, singing French
tongues, wine numbed mismatched thrusts, bent
beat love. Love was moon poetry quilled through
love vapors, lost like a slipper to emerging dawns.
Time finds her exhuming that spring to sweeten a
soured tongue—remembering gooseflesh skin in the
evening chill. Parked away from memory of sister's
pregnant belly beating out a warning to lovers
pressing the mildewed mattress. Still in their boots
that first time; jeans rolled low, out in the peach
orchard—near Slaughterhouse Sluice—a catfish hole
where the likely catch was heifer's blood surfacing
like Easter egg dye against a water spider's dance.

At Lookout Point

in spite of bucket seats,
we honeyed our iguana tongues
as apple twisted dark limbs
on rumps of green
wrapped in blankets of arms
watched the valley turn an electric dusk.

Track Talk

She has the look of a thoroughbred
with a high-heeled gait.
I know better.
She races on numbered sheets
at downs silvered by moons.
She won't race unless
he feeds her gold carrots,
guides her in dancing shoes
with diamond bridles.
She wears a wild mane,
says it's a natural rein
only warriors can grasp.

Secretly he's been looking for a buyer.
Lately she can't shake the scent of stallion—
blames: lineage, Grandmother's unlatched
stable gate, Grandfather's mustang blood
won't let her run a straight eastern track
with all those western ranges
waiting to be explored.

Remembering Louise

For Christmas she gave him
a hanging pot

dripping Purple Passion.
He gave it to me the spring
she railed from Toronto to Seattle.

I let the passion die and kept the pot.

Chapter 3 **Sock Relations**

A Lucky Girl

She is the youngest daughter,
the good listener,
the lucky one with straight
teeth, the last born,
not often given to advice.
People tell her their secrets.

Before dad ran off to Mexico,
with the best friend,
the older sister never had
much to say about life at *Farmlands*:
the high-water bungalow,
twenty-acres of tomatoes,
stewing in summer's kettle.
How she skips right through his warnings
Don't go down to the river.

Never speaks of the whippings,
behind the barn,
except to the little sister,
the good listener.
How it takes forever to unhook his belt,
the one with the horseshoe buckle.

How she braces for the sting
against the planks of bubbled paint,
leather to soft skin
tattoed with welts
as if she just stepped on a wasp's nest,
and not out of line.

Children Are Like Rivers

when you try to straighten them out
they might go along with you for awhile
then they'll jump their banks
to snatch back their wild.
All you really have to do is:
widen their boundaries
and let them meander.

Middle Age Lament

You know you are middle-aged when you look into
the mirror, plagued by confusion, focus your trifocals
and realize it's *not* your mother in the reflection when
the cashier remarks that you have a beautiful grand-
daughter, but you're with your daughter, the bag clerk
refers to you as *Ma'am* as she offers to help you and
your groceries to the car.

You know you are middle-aged while staying under
your allotted Weight Watchers points, the scales
maintain you gained five pounds. You tell yourself
they must be broken and jog extra laps around the
park, then need to see a sports doctor.

You know you are middle-aged when an ideal Friday
night is to order Kung Pao Chicken, stream a movie,
only to fall asleep in your Barcalounger, to wake at six
a.m. with a stiff-neck. You really hope there's a God
and a heaven, as you bump into your parents, who live
with you now, and have just beat you to the bathroom.

You know you are middle-aged when your husband
O.D's on Palmetto and Viagra and your choice of rec-
reational drugs is Ginkgo Biloba, Coenzyme Q10
and that medical marijauna. You know you're middle-aged
because it is 30 degrees outside and you are sweating
in short sleeves and have a craving for tofu.

You know because you mistook your son's teacher for his classmate and your colleague's date for his daughter. Why else is your daughter wearing *your* reincarnated bell bottoms and Elton John's platform shoes?
And you wouldn't need to buy sensible shoes from *The Walking Store.*

But you are middle-aged and so what if you are walking slower-at least you are walking. So what if your kids think you were born before the Dark Ages instead of having survived the Age of Aquarius.

Grandma Bessie

i.

Grandma worked
at the packing shed,
left school after eighth-grade
when more hands were needed for the dairy,
took her place next to her mother
squatting on stools coaxing milk
from sour faced cows,
loved to write stories.

Gave it up after marriage
to a man with ambition,
camping in an army tent
at her brother's orange grove
saving money for *their* dairy.

They grew to hate the cows,
sold everything after he
bluffed his way through
his third-grade education
into a line foreman at Harter's cannery.

ii.

You'd never know
she'd just chopped off hen's head,
was on her hands and knees
picking strawberries big as apples,
knew her way around the Smith and Wesson—
a better shot than her husband.

Was a lady who hadn't
married someone with
no iota about business,
wore her best suit to town
pinned with rhinestones,
cocked the feathered hat just so,
clutched the pocketbook
with smooth gloved hands,
to cover her calluses.

Sock Relations

Your grandpa wore white cotton socks summers,
grey woolens winters.
Your grandma balled his socks
darned holes Thompson's toes poked through.
They stayed mated.
Your ma married a man wore
white cottons and grey woolens.
The marriage endured.
You married a man wore Orlon,
knotted his socks—kept a spare drawer
with lost mates.
The marriage was a mismatch.
Your new man's got himself a darnin' egg
and doesn't ask you to mend what his livin' wears out.

Three Questions to a Daughter

• Why did you leave?

Time won't wait. I was born to fly away—open your
hand—that is all it will carry. I wanted a room to fill
with success, mistakes, jumble of drawers brimmed
with scarves from Paris and Hampton Court, promise
of love, my mess, my order a quiet place.

• Why did you leave with a musician?

His music plays in the key that unlocks my heart.

• Why have you chosen this drafty Victorian—rooms
  without furniture, stubborn windows that once open,
  refuse to close, a temperamental stove, lack of heat?

The rooms are furnished with light, through the win-
dows float the delta breeze that chimes the ancient
elms—his arms are the only blanket I need, I grow fat
on love—because this is enough.

Sweet Sixteen

She was sixteen
sweet sixteen
young woman
young radiant woman
sunlight pouring from
every pore of a woman
smile larger than the moon,
inviting like an open hand
sweet child barely jumped
from her mama's womb

jumped off her Daddy's knee
practicing at being a woman
sweet child with autumn hair and skin
the summer flecked gold
found her way to the Yuba
Maidu call the place of mourning

where children play with
grown-up toys-Broncos and Cherokees
on the warm days
drink beer, cut school
bask in peach perfume
sky deep wells of blue

the river that in winters of too much rain
climbs its banks
swift in spring with winter melt
purposeful
coaxed by Mara, mother sea

beneath the surface calm
hunger mouths of sinkholes
muscled undertow
easy to swallow
snags: saplings, SUVs, boys and girls

I dream you rise
fly wet blood and bones
shake off the cold
release notes as smooth as river stones
follow the geese home.

Conversations

I asked the sky if it defined
the boundary of the barn.
Sky replied,"Trust what is seen,
answer all else with faith."

The barn said, "I sit on the earth,
a shelter made from the limbs of a sister oak,
older than I and who once held up the sky."
The spirit of the sister oak said to the barn,
"The sky was never a burden
even resting on my shoulders."

Her son called to the passing squirrel,
"I welcome you across my threshold
as friends do pilgrims, mothers their children."
The squirrel thanked Father Lightning
for opening a door.

A hawk flying by called down,
"If you agree there are no differences
between endings and beginnings,
no boundary will define you."
Then the wind came up, whispering,
"In each breath reside all answers."

Prayers

After the cancer spreads
surgeons remove an arm
he beats his wife with
the one that remains
gets religion,
begs forgiveness.
But it is the widow's prayers
that are answered.

The Apron

Her mother's gift
frayed lace,
pretty
faded floral print,
stray bleach stain;
tied with a flourish
around a waist
she's battled for years.

Shields favorite jeans, T-shirts,
going-out-kicking-up-her-heals-skirts,
holiday vests,
what it could not:
the wound over her heart,
a first husband the cemetery keeps,
sons to the Iraq War,
a daughter married too soon,
one given to drink.

Holds what the day offers:
lost toys, zinnias' red heads, tears,
stray kittens, a finch's repose
cell phones, winter greens,
toddlers sticky fingers,
what she finds
what's left behind.

First Harvest

Before the skies pepper with fowl
the first hard freeze she climbs the knoll
booted feet the muddy road
complaint of knees
basket slung on flannelled arm
the farmwoman's charm bracelet

Fog cobwebs the orchard
noon sun brooms away
surveys a family's labor
a daughter's inheritance

She chooses Mirabelles, Bartlett, Anjous, Bosc
for their fragrance: honey and spice
imperfect skins conceal pale sweet flesh
chooses for color: lutescent coppery, sumac red,
those blushed by summer's constant gaze
for their song of curves

for how they fill an empty hand.

Do What My Brothers Got to Do

When I was ten I wanted to
do what my brothers got to do:
kill things living or dead,
bucks,
does,
piles of rocks,
gophers,
beer bottles
hook trout,
catfish and their finger,
spit lugies,
burn rubber on the John Deere,
be waited on by the women,
drink grandpa's whiskey, grimace,
start fights in the parking lot of
the Pump House Bar
try to kick the cat,
smoke Marlboros,
shout four letter words,
leave dirty underwear on the floor,
get grease under my nails, in my teeth and hair
replacing a carbonator,
drive without a license—whistle real loud.

Number 69

July we go to Gertrude Stein's grave. Take the number 69
to the Père Lachaise Cemetery—la cite des mort. Forget-
ting the bundle of stones drop handfuls of gratitude. We
imagine a massive edifice chiseled with verse as impress-
ive as she was; nothing grows at Jim Morrison's grave, the
earth hard packed by tourists' spent cigarettes, empty
cartons of take away, faded roses. We follow the map past
photos of family plots: Louis, Du Bois, surnames buried
beneath Irish and Germans in America. My daughter
poses for pictures with petals of violet eyes, says she hates
to smile. The cemetery is quiet except for the larks, never
without a word. If I lived in Paris, this is where I'd picnic,
sketch, neck, nap. At our flat in Le Marais I write poems
to my father who'd marched the Champs-Élysées a hero,
now gone over a decade—memory powerful, magic like
an Alice Hoffman novel, sudden notes of chimes in prac-
ticed hands of wind, a baby's downy head—lightness of a
body floating at the lake. I see him in his cabin skin and
bones—hold my breath—if I don't he'll blow away.

Before We Had Breasts

grandmother tried to reel

us in with the hook of her tongue,

afraid we'd drown

swimming the backstroke

slicing waves of milky meringue

flaked with driftwood.

Free-styled to deep water.

Floated chests pressed

to blue domes of sky.

Propellers of feet

in lemon light

beneath logs of sugar pine

tied with ribbons of steel

surprising catfish, big as dogs.

Fly Fishing

Grandfather was a patient teacher.
There was no more gifted orator
on the fly, trade secrets
netted in her braids,
tucked beneath a straw hat
with the marabou jig.

Summers he'd demonstrate the way
to bait a hook, when to troll,
with the right bait:
nymphs, dillys, Velveeta.
Follow the moon's phases,
leading to the deepest pools,
catch and release what needed
to lengthen another season.

She gave up the pole
never getting her limit,
reel in the elusive lunger,
fishing in ponds of words,
streams of consciousness,
following in his footsteps,

another pursuit that cannot be rushed.

Rite of Passage

If you listen to the basket
you'll hear the footsteps
of the Weaver
gathering weft of Panyúrara grass,
willow, Five Finger Fern,
wild grape, tule for color
adornments of Wolf Moss,
and porcupine quills.

On our tenth fall grandma took us
to a cabin sitting on the edge
of the Madeline Plains
at the base of a pine covered butte
where she'd waded, as a girl,
up to her waist in sage
its scent rushing
through the open cabin door,
like a heady woman, medicine woman
burning a smudge stick.

Grandma's backyard stretched
farther then she could run,
basket in hand, collecting obsidian
shiny and black as her eyes
set in the sandy floor of a Jurassic sea,
jewels to a child who had none.
By day my brother and Grandma
walked the plains hunting sage hens.
I stayed close to the cabin,
carried water from the spring
drew myself into pictures of cityscapes.
knew I would never be a hunter,
preferred the music of silence,

broken by the movement,
of cabin rats playing percussion in the attic.

One afternoon, at the spring,
I shared a drink with a porcupine.
Never telling my brother,
too trigger happy to keep a secret.
Now, I live in the city
paint myself into landscapes,

This is not really an escape—
nor as good as that drink at the spring.
What does this have to do with baskets?
They hold the harvest.
Let's just say this poem is a basket,
keeping the gift of memory.

Enlightened Version of Death

"You do not go to heaven when you die. You get stiffer
than a Brillo pad, smell worse than grandma's compost
pile (unless they pickle you) and look dead unless
they powder and rouge you. Then, you are either
buried six feet deep, just close enough to the devil's
furnace to keep you warm, or the mortals cast your
burnt remains to an indifferent heaven that drops you
back to earth quicker than Newton's apple or you end
up like Uncle Harry—in the marble urn on Aunt
Orvella's mantel by the photograph he hated. And
after you are dead you go on living because while
you're living you leave pieces of yourself with every-
one you touch gently or crossly so, you best live your
life accordingly."

The Matter of His Remains

He asked his sister, asked a fifth wife
and a favorite daughter
to tend to his remains.
This, the last wife, wasn't legal
but true in heart.
They'd exchanged vows in San Blas
at the little church in the plaza
though he was still married to the fourth wife--
left it to God to judge.

It would be just two women in the burial party
who waited for the daughter fidgeting
with their wedding bands nuisances
paddling a canoe to the middle
of the lake, at 7 a.m.
parting curtains of mist
that ruin their hair:
one head curls corkscrews
the other flattens straight as flax.
When the sister opens the cedar box
 ashes spoil the morning's make-up.
So that even now he gets the last word.

On shore they both mourn differently:
one takes shots of Jim Beam
the other prays to Jesus.
The pebbly beach soon is buoyant
with children's laughter carried up
the canyon on piney winds.
Sailboats shatter the mirrored water,
no bad luck follows.
Fishing reels hum.
Trout arc toward turquoise dragonflies.

Still no sign of the daughter,
a dreamer believing what is
and what seems are often the same
whose wrong turn sees her go missing.

Dream Memory

"Your mother will not be with us long,"
says the river with no name
that feeds the pond,
"The fowl take flight in round full song."

She thinks of her mother
in the small room with
varnished floors
white washed walls
spooned in honey light
old wounds split open
to dark hunger.

"This is normal," says the woman
who lives with a peacock at the pond.
"Reach in your throat for the missing language
that speaks to the part stretching in all directions.
Follow the gauze of stars,
to moons sweet enough to eat."

Paper Prisoner

Yesterday they delivered the new chairs,
blue to match my mood.
I would rather have a window, or clean building air,
but they tell me, "Be satisfied with your
executive blue chair. With a six inch padded seat
how deep you will sink and never want
to leave this trendy room."
Mauve decor can't hide the fact it's still a cell
and I'm a paper prisoner with paper clip chains
terminally down, tame as the African violet on my desk
blooming under unnatural light,
where managers pace the halls
sporting polyester smiles.
Noontime, I flee to the K Street Mall,
prisoner to the yard.
I do not plan escape-hop light-rail,
tunnel the paperwork;
I only want to exercise.
I am not hungry like this man on the steps
of the Cathedral of the Blessed Sacrament,
wearing three dirty shirts, a grin,
last night's *Thunderbird*.
I wear silk, expensive perfume, and weak regret.
I am overweight, live for the next state holiday,
and have never seriously considered parole.
I turn my head down wind
drop a dollar in his palm as he *God blesses* me.

Screen Saver

Monday Morning
planted in front of the computer screen,
a bad seed,
fenced in a 4 by 5 foot cubicle
alert to the plodding tremor, the supervisor's gait
christened secretly as "Big Bird"
whose vocabulary is limited to...
"Shouldn't, Wouldn't, Can't."
After she lopes away
I meditate on the screen saver
A daughter: defiant smile
framed between dimpled cheeks
batting pigtails like whips
in faded blue jeans
one raised fist
shoeless at the river bank
reminding me that sometimes
you need to play dirty.

Chapter 4   **Accidental Habitat**

Dawn in Senlis

A compress of rain breaks the fever
wind bells the beech leaves,
the moon unmoored
floats with last stars
light of Venus the orange of Mars,
cobbled streets shiny as onyx,
smooth as river stones sanded
by a thousand years of soles.

Churches cold as a deep freeze
welcome reprieve from summer heat
for the woman in the pew
Mary leaks hope.

Outside the market opens
from shuttered vans
vendors unload Spanish limes,
Indian linens, Moroccan silver.
A man in a red bandana offers baguettes
halved Charentis melons
stringy as brains.

She passes lovers locked in embrace,
hollyhocks, crepe paper petals dark as cabernet
bloom in impossible space,
Augustus' privileged stare
missing part of his nose,
at war with the elements since the 5th Century.

An Accidental Habitat

Two mallards, a husband and wife,
have taken up residence in the park
with the crows and hawks poised
in watchful grace.
What are the draws?
Firearms prohibited signs—
a concrete pond, nobody is using?

We watch their waddle
toward the water
return to the green
after the sprinklers shut off
and armies of angle worms
surface for air.

The couple rejoice
in this impromptu marsh
flap napkins of wings,
feast.

I Am the Creek

slow and easy
in this fall of *Han Lu*
mother of minnow
swimming in nursery schools
sleeping in cradles
of algae and sedge

dance floor
to Damselflies
gyration of blue unions
to the tambourine of leaves

tomb to families of oak
anointed in my waters
last rites repeated
in the currents' passage

riparian spring
to hare and fox
drunk in the tent of dusk
and the apricot light
of a *Samhain* moon.

the place of wading
into muddy beginnings
and pools of clarity
changing my course often
lithe as the water snake's glide.

The Heron

meditates on the ripple
in the dredge pond,
recites the mantra
of the bluegill,
spears only thoughts
releases these,
practices a patient religion.

Amaryllis Belladonna, Beautiful Lady

You bloom in winter
on coffee tables
in kitchen windows
root in loam
float in glassy pools
ascend toward milky light

when others
shutter up to seed
swathed in golden quilts
swallow winter's tonic—dream of spring,
you, flower
a South African Queen
carmine petticoats of lips.

The wait worth your smile.

Lines from a Zen Poem

Eve posed the question to the universe:
"How can I think-non-thinking?"

The silence answered, "Speak with a broad tongue
and the wind will bring the water's voice to your pillow
the moon shadow of oaks through open windows
and the mind, dreams with
the truth of grass, trees, pebbles,
wind, rain, water and fire.

If first the meaning is unclear
you have only to drink the knowledge
at wells of sunshine
splash in rain of the stars' light.
wear clothes fashioned from heaven and earth.

Then you will dwell in a place of constant summer."

American Beauties

Your mothers tell lies
made their bargains
I come with clippers

your angled stems
poised in my water prisons
on polished tables
blossom winning smiles

the pageant over
you'll return
a dark magic
shoveled into May gardens

to blow the French horns of zucchinis
sugar summer tomatoes
wave flags of sweet peas
raise shields of sunflowers
plump the orange moon pumpkins.

Human Nature

We live in the sky, not under it.
But our logic stunts our wings
forever bound to the
nest of mediocrity.
Unable to take flight, we dig in
even when it is not in our interest
cry to be fed
like the newborn crested sparrows
cradled in the cedar
never full
nudging siblings
to be the first
to glean
the fat worm.

Twenty Signs of a Cold Winter

sparrows chirp under full moons
dogs' hair thickens at the nape of their necks
cats refuse to go outside
roses drop false blooms
grey mouths of sky
swallow dark fruit of crows
spiders nest in corners of the house
crickets appear on the hearths
pigs gather sticks
there is an abundance of acorns
pipes burst before they can be wrapped
dreams lengthen
heavy fogs in August
frequent halos around the sun
we take to bed earlier and wake later
raccoons sport bright bands
rats strum the rafters
we crave brandy in spiced cider
cheeks ripen in the morning chills
ants drink from kitchen faucets
mice raid Hoosier cabinets.

Two Dawns and One Afternoon in Tierra Buena

Barefoot
night gown a jellyfish of north wind
drifting over frozen alfalfa fields
alone with the dark blur of crows
and a cock pheasant stirred to flight
colliding with a bruised dawn.

4 a.m. chasing down county road 39A
the moon flinging silver threads of light
illuminating something you can't hold or lose
promises between two best friends.
Sworn to secrecy on the Methodist bible's
thinning leather cover
binding pages of overused proverbs
to the aperture in the privet hedge
where in the spring
white crowned sparrows nest
as this night
we did.

The barn smelled of hay and chicken shit
stood standing when everything else
came down from neglect
including
childhood one afternoon
drenched in Carmel light
the bite of a zipper's teeth
catching skin
the unexpected
bloom of red.

August Moon

All night the moon danced
partnered with stars
honey blushed
foiled in silver
leaves at dawn
led by the warm hands of sun.

Fifty Days and Fifty Nights

Mid-winter grass brown as late August hills
ancient camellias familiar to change
leak crimson on dark gauze of leaves
mild weather false springs
sudden freezes usher hunger moons
January daffodils tie March bonnets
magnolias stir to silent bees
Lady Bugs forget to winter over
Turtle doves' pleated wings warm winter nests.

The bone barometer registers rain
incantations answered
high pressure implodes
to frenzied crows
dogs roll into furry balls
dream of downpours
drought melts.

Adaptation

Trout swim toward the stars
imagine nymphs
in vapored air—
is the kingfisher's dive,
finless swimmer
blind to limitations.

Trio

i.

Sound chalice
incised with tongues
blood stained
born of darkness
green notes fastened to
rungs of light.

ii.

Here with robins'
lifting twigs
through sodden air
clouds of gnats
all one song.

iii.

I ask morning if
there is a poem in the
sparrows' hedge
lemon cupped narcissus
brimmed with steady rain
in the iris releasing
fists of bruised blooms.

Blessing

Blessed with a blossoming heart
with summer flowers seeded in spring
in this garden of wild, native, exotic, and tame;
this pitcher of morning light
poured across the wooden planks
Canas' umbrella of leaves;
the walnut's basket of nuts
squirrels' steady harvest
mandalas of black-eyed Susan fringed in gold
sycamores and breeze linked in song.

Blessed with sparrows' passion to sing,
humming birds' endurance, inquisitive jays,
afternoon baptisms' quiver of wings
release of sorrow
space that cultivates joy;
feelings turned over
like the trowel amends;
the yin yang
sadness and joy
different and the same.

Juggler of Fire

I'm
surprised by the
moon a yellow Frisbee
caught in the open hand of sky
above Notre Dame's square
the man juggling fire
crowds that mushroom
fireworks raining down
not Walt Disneyish or Pixarish
intense bang bang
when the man tames the fire
everyone claps
bone to bone.

Jongleur de Feu

Je suis
supris par la
frisbee lune un Frisbee jaune
pris dans la main ouverte du ciel
ci-dessus place Notre-Dame de
le feu jonglerie home
foules qui augmentent
feux d'artifice a pleuvoiir
pas Walt Disneyish ou Pixarish
intense bang bang
quand Phomme apprivoise le feu
taut le monde applaudit
osseuse a l'os.

Impromptu Prophet

Behind the Arco Station
the homeless man makes
a breakfast of mustard greens
and Miner's lettuce
growing in the open field
the city hasn't tamed.
He pounds the greens on
the improvised
cutting board of curb
deposits the mash into
a cup of steaming water
improbable gourmet,
impromptu prophet who says,
"The meaning of life is:
a sunny day, a field of greens
a cup of hot water that the kid
at Starbucks gives away
for free."

Footpath from Vernon to Giverny

The path mimes the curvature of the Seine
pauses at Le Vieux Moulin
brigades of hollyhock
chartreuse corollas
the bees attend
collecting pistil's powder
past Château des Tourelles
with its gunners of swallows
barrels of dark wings
Monet's fields,
red poppies
black holes
fed on fingers of light.

Spring Proverb

She carries home spring
honey bees sting
lips of redbud
pressed to cheeks of sky
mushrooms tipping crimson caps
golden bowls of sun
wild onion salted tears
Miner's lettuce
the toll of White Bells
mustard greens overflowing
platters of fields
careful not to bite off
more than she can chew
forage with intention
take only what she'll use
because one still starves
with a basket full of dirt.

Zelda Incarnate

Poised at the hearth, paws of snow
in the cottage veneered in sepia light
spark of chestnut eyes
mink coat streaked gold
thump of bushy tail.

Children's voices once cheered this room
lost to accidents in the field,
progress, its hum of mills, cholera,
ships oversea to farm America
only the old stay.

You fill the void, shepherd sheep
bark down dangers mute to human ears
keep safe the fowl from feral cat and fox
night fall, blanket the farm folks' feet.

The cast iron pot simmers soup
kitchen garden roots
yesterday's bone
rosemary and thyme, balm the air.

At first light your mistress rolled yeasty bread
that rose and fell temperamental as fall
baked golden slices tenderness
butters the husband's round, one for you
the patient beggar a penchant for buttery fingers.

Glad you no longer stray
find a good home in this Dutch painting

in the Age of Discovery on the museum wall,
proof spirits travel, transcend, reincarnate
beyond chasing park balls, frightening the mail carrier
I miss your wet nose
herding the errant human
with kindly patience.

Living in Chapters of a Novel

Stained glass bleeds watery light.
Mary's forgiving smile
rests upon the heretic seated in the pew.
In this heat wave out of Africa
only churches cold as root cellars bring respite.
I've come to find Princess Judith,
come to write her a way out of the
monastery in Senlis
walk slate stones polished by her feet,
find my niche like
hollyhock blooms
between cottage and rue,
seach her out at the marché,
crowding narrow streets
purchase pastel cottons sure to shrink
pointy Moroccan shoes that pinch the toes,
shoulder length earrings,
to please the princess, buy two.

Three Buddhists

I.

She was a dancer surrounded by space in an apartment,
above a tailor who turned off the heat when he left his
shop for the day. The air was so cold her breath made
clouds. Chianti bottles pooled with candle wax on
hardwood floors. Her name was Jilang. She was preg-
nant but only a little. She had eyes the same as Angel
Fish always surprised with spidery lashes that made a
breeze. Tuesdays she went to a house where there were
small silk pillows that people knelt upon to talk to their
beads. Everyone welcomed her with even smiles. After
prayer they ate butter cookies and drank herbal teas.
She'd married a bass player who was either on coke or
on tour. She was going home as soon as she started to
show.

II.

She'd studied art, was never athletic, never had stam-
ina, but was swimming from her life, a husband in a
house drowning in Periwinkle. In this house slate-
skinned lizards drank water from kitchen faucets.
They'd play dead, motionless in the enamel basin their
dark eyes dots of fear. She got jobs teaching schizo-
phrenics to draw self-portraits in facilities where every
door locked behind her. One day out of the blue, she
offered me a cat with little white boots, which walked
right into my house and sat down in my favorite chair.
This cat taught itself to knock at the door and her kit-
tens to do the same. She didn't want the cat because she
was bringing home her baby. She'd turned her laundry

room into a nursery, papering the walls with the cow-jumped-over-the-moon motif and borders of stars. I gave the baby a carousel of farm animals that spun around playing " Old McDonald's Farm" that never failed to make the baby sleep. Neither of us could know these things before they came to be.

III.

Her mandalas demanded to know what their colors meant, how she felt after drawing them, raised questions: why she'd forgiven her parents but not her first husband and so on. When she opened her drawing book the pages wailed. She drew imperfect circles without a compass, filled them with images, words, and color: Prussian blue, Crimson, Hooker green. The images wrote poetry. The tongue sang to the world and the world swallowed the words and began again.

The Seattle Salmon Tea Rose (#F6666)

Energy forced this play
its balanced mix of carotenoids
cued by nature's understudies;
enough water, the wrong time
temperatures of unseasonable degree.

The tea rose stays in character,
not to be upstaged
by an empty house,
January suns suspended
from ceilings of fog
spotlight a minimalist stage
its leafless props
devoid of their audience of bees.

She
delivers her soliloquy
not unlike you or I, in
our own out of sync performances
blooming to false springs.

The Sunflowers in My Garden

In the sea
I might mistake you for anemones
on the savannah, cousins to the giraffes
in my garden, dancers with
sunny dispositions
yellow tongues lap the wind
leggy lines of green tights
layers of leafy crinolines
lift
crowns of dark seed
balanced on long necks
following the slant of rays
bowing your heads late September.

Notes

"Pas de Deux." – An ekphrasis poem inspired by William Theophilus Brown's *Figures in the Field*.

"Sweet Sixteen" – This poem is dedicated to my neice, Haley Maria Marshall, who transcended this earth at sixteen.

"First Harvest" – An ekphrasis poem inspired by Renaldo Cuneo's *Pears*.

"Matter of His Remains – "a dreamer believing what is and what seems are often the same" are lines from "The Bells of San Blas" by Henry Wadsworth Longfellow.

"I Am the Creek" – Han Lu is Chinese season of cold dew and Samhain is the Celtic Autumn Equinox Celebration.

"Trio" – Inspired after reading a series of Eugenio Montale's poems.

"Juggler of Fire"–Translation is by Aubrey Pickering

"Zelda Incarnate"– An ekphrasis poem inspired by the John Albertus Neuhuys' painting, *Afternoon Snack in the Farmhouse*.

"Sunflowers in My Garden"– Inspired after reading Mary Oliver's "The Sunflower."

Jennifer O'Neill Pickering grew up in Tierra Buena and Yuba City, California and lived in Buffalo, New York.

She is a featured poet and essayist at the online website, *Restore and Restory: A Peoples History of the Cache Creek Nature Preserve*. "I Am the Creek" was selected, with seven other poets, for the site-specific sculpture, *Open Circle*, in Sacramento, CA. Other publication credits include: *Sacramento Voices* (2014,) Poet*News* (interviews and poetry), *Tiger's Eye Journal* (poetry), *Cosumnes River Journal, Heresies*, (New York City) and *Yellow Silk* (Oakland, CA).

At an early age she was drawn to visual and literary art and studied art and writing at S.U.N.Y. Buffalo and then later received an MA in Studio Art at C.S.U. Sacramento. She is a graduate of the Artist Residency Institute for both visual and literary arts that was sponsored by the Sacramento Metropolitan Arts Commission. Her award-winning visual art is featured in *Moon Mist Valley, 13th Moon* (S.U.N.Y. Albany), *Poetsexpresso*, *News & Review*, *Cosumnes River Journal*, *Sacramento Bee*, and other publications. *Blue Moon Literary & Art Journal*, and *13th Moon* (S.U.N.Y. Albany) feature her visual art on their covers. Her art, Summer Garden Spirit, was also, selected for the poster in the exhibit, *Creating Freedom: The Art and Poetry of Domestic Violence Survivors* at the California History Museum.

Jennifer's visual art has been exhibited in many Sacramento galleries including: The Verge, Poets' Gallery, Fe Gallery, Davis Art Center, Crocker Art Museum, Robert Else Gallery CSU Sacramento, California History Museum, CSU Sacramento Annex Gallery in the traveling show: *PTSD Nation*, Capitol Public Radio, S.U.N.Y. Buffalo, KVIE Public Television, Channel 10 News and the Sacramento Bee.

In 2013, she was awarded a grant from the Sacramento Metropolitan Arts Commission to compile and edit the anthology entitled, *Sable & Quill: The visual art and writing of writers who are also artists*. Awards include the best California State Workers Poem and honorable mention for a collection of poems and short stories, entitled, "The Farmlands Stories," *Five Quarterly*. Her prose piece, the" Improbable Cat Lover" was published by Harlequin in *The Dog with the Old Soul*.

On occasion she combines the two mediums of visual and literary art in the form of mixed media art and handmade books.

While working as a Technology Specialist for the State of California, some of her photography and graphic designs appeared on these websites: State of California Assembly California State Senate Chaplain, and the California State Capitol Museum.

Jennifer has taught in many public venues including: Cosumnes River College, the public libraries, schools and at St. John's Shelter for Women and Children.

She makes her home in Sacramento, California where she writes, gardens and makes art. Contact the author at Jennifer's Art and Words on her blog at:*http://jenniferword.blogspot.com/* and *Jenniferartist@gmail.com.*

www.ingramcontent.com/pod-product-compliance
Lightning Source LLC
Chambersburg PA
CBHW041103110426
42740CB00043B/142